UNCOMPLICATED

A Guide to Thriving in the Corporate World

Basak Gunaydin

www.TotalPublishingAndMedia.com

I dedicate this book to my mother, Efser,
For her unwavering love and support and unlimited
imagination that all things are possible.

ACKNOWLEDGEMENTS

No one does anything on their own. It does take a village or in my case, many wise teachers, friends, bosses, colleagues, my mother, and my husband. I need to single out a few for their help in creating this book.

My dear friend, partner in yoga, Katherine Hall, who has been my editor and consultant. English being my second language, she has been my guide; tirelessly correcting my grammar mistakes, creating a welcoming space to run ideas by, to discuss sentence structures with, and putting me on deadlines. Without her, this book would not be what it is. Gratitude from the bottom of my heart. Everyone needs a partner in whatever they do, like Kate!

My first boss in New York, who I consider my "American Father", Barry Finn. I have been enormously lucky to be taken under the wings by someone like Barry, who believed in me, taught me, travelled with me, and gave me a second job, replacing himself as he retired. He fought with me and loved me. His contribution to my career and who I became is most tremendous.

And finally, my teacher, Yogi Charu. Meeting him at a time in my life when I was slightly tired of my job, searching for answers about life, purpose and meaning, has been the most precious gift. Studying with Yogi Charu, made a big impact on my personal life and as an extension to my business life. His teachings have given me clarity, serenity, peace and harmony within myself and my environment. I found the answers I have been looking for under His tutorship. I am grateful for him –a lifetime teacher and a friend.

WHY READ THIS BOOK?

This is a well-thought out and helpful book for anyone, who is:

- Starting out in their Career
- Wishing to get a better job
- Wanting to be happier at a current job
- Desiring to influence their mood and attitude, regardless of current employment
- Interested in a different perspective and a philosophy which supports their wellbeing

FOREWORD

Basak has worked with me to transform all aspects of my life. With her guidance as a life coach and her abundant positive energy, I have come to a greater understanding of myself and my potential. A shift in our mental space is always reflected in our reality. As such, I have witnessed positive changes in my career and my personal life, and most importantly as a soul on this spiritual journey. Basak's diligent self-practice in the beautiful Vedic culture of philosophy and yoga enriches her life. With that, she can comfortably offer to touch and nurture other lives. I've never met anyone with such bright and vibrant positivity. Once you meet Basak, you will want to be a person of kind. That energy is reflected in the many useful ideas and practices in this book. Perhaps you, too, are seeking a way to uncover your unique power and thus uncomplicate your life. If so, I urge you to read on....

Luyan Noelle Dai
Measurement Product Specialist
@Google, Singapore

Having been guiding people across the globe in wellness, mental health, relaxation, yoga, and philosophical thinking for the last three decades, I have encountered variety of clients from all walks of life. When I Moved to New York, thirteen years ago, Basak was one of the students I met early on. I worked with Basak since then through many trainings; meditation, breathwork, philosophy to name a few.

When I first met Basak she was a successful businesswoman in the Fashion world. She would be travelling around the planet from Monday to Friday and be back in the city Friday evening to partake in the trainings all weekend. She then began teaching Relaxation and meditation to the staff of her company and other corporate groups around the world. I have seen Basak transition from the corporate world to become a fulltime spiritual guide, life coach, yoga, and meditation teacher to all rounds of life including the corporate world that she knows best.

It is no coincidence that a book like this has manifested itself. The wisdom and practices that you will find in this lotus like gem have helped the author in living a more balanced life. Striving to be the best in both the business and the spiritual practices, her humble realizations can only affect the reader in bringing balance in their life which is a lovely need in today's hectic world. Enjoy!

Yogi Charu

"Disciple of the Saraswati lineage, one of the ten classical monk orders in India founded by Adi Sankaracharya in the 8th century. Yogi Charu was inducted into this lineage by Anandakapila Saraswati, a celebrated author on Tantra and Kriya yoga."

How This Book Is Organized

This book is organized in progressing chapters addressing various situations and circumstances in the workplace.

Should you choose to use it as a guidebook, there are "how to" guides that give quick instructions or if you wish to delve deeper, a theory behind these bullet points and real-life scenarios supporting them are available for the reader. There are practices the reader can do which are both easy and effective to practice, in these different circumstances.

Chapters progress as follows:

Chapter 1: A fresh perspective in being empowered to look for a new job

Chapter 2: Interview process for both interviewee and interviewer

Chapter 3: How to show up the first days at work, to set your future with the organization

TABLE OF CONTENTS

INTRODUCTION

You are a ruby embedded in granite.
How long will you pretend it's not true?
We can see it in your eyes.
Come to the root of the root of your Self
~ Rumi

We are constantly negotiating the balance between work and well-being in our lives. We learn how to "do" our jobs, but no one teaches us how to "be" our whole self in the workplace. Some of us sacrifice the path of self-discovery and the nurturing of our individuality, in an effort to "fit in" and "not stand out," while others climb to the top at the expense of the health of their mind and body. We are not taught the value of our uniqueness and how to cultivate an inner connection which brings us happiness and helps us find our mission in life – allowing us to thrive in what we do. As a result, most of us "survive" the workplace and push through until our bodies and or mental energies are exhausted, our spirits broken.

Recent research on" Study Finds" say 64% of American workers are fearful of being authentic around others at work. Seven in ten say they adopt an entirely different personality when they are at work, compared to their normal persona at home. According to Forbes, a study by Careerbuilder.com shows a whopping 58% percent of managers said they did not receive management training. Imagine that! Most managers in the workplace were promoted because they were good at their jobs but not necessarily good at leading and inspiring people around them. Yet another study done by MetLife, in 2022, revealed 72% of employers say stress and/or burn out are a challenge and or a concern for their organization. All these studies point to the overwhelming dysfunction in companies, where historically employee well-being is ignored or sacrificed for the bottom line. Companies are just beginning to understand the importance of supporting the mental health of their employees.

As Companies explore the dynamics in "employee focused" strategies, there is an opportunity to become aware of employee's well-being, holistically. Corporate leaders need to learn how to create healthy models of behavior, by adopting a deeper dive into human psyche and stop rushing around to "get things done". They need to slow down and become more intuitive, inquisitive, and observant of themselves and others. As awareness is cultivated in this way, employees will feel more connected to their inner and outer environment.

This is what is in the heart of yoga. In our Western understanding yoga is a type of physical exercise, but this in essence is only 1/8th of what yoga really is, as described in Patanjali's 8 limbs of yoga. Fundamental purpose of yoga is to foster harmony in the mind, body, and environment to release mental, emotional and physical suffering which is inherit in human experience. As the tension in the mind and body is released, there is a deeper connection to our innermost nature and true purpose. As a yoga therapist, I work with the clients and students by applying Yogic principles with the objective of achieving a particular spiritual, psychological, or physiological goal.

We all have a unique reason why we turn to spirituality. Mine was a combination of being in distress and seeking knowledge. I arrived in New York City from Turkey, a twenty-three-year-old recent Textile Engineer graduate going to work for an apparel company. I was young and dealing with cultural and language differences. After a thirty-year career, traveling the world, being the youngest manager, later the only female leader in the boardroom I have achieved a certain amount of traditional success. I lived up to the expectations and often surpassed them by dedicating my life to my work, finding my way through trial and errors. But all of this came with frustration and challenges, and eventually I learned that none of this so-called success equaled happiness. I had great mentors along the way, but no one taught me how to take care of myself and not lose the connection with my essence. So, I began to question. By taking time for self-healing, self-study, yoga and meditation trainings, and absorbing the wisdom of some great teachers along the way, I was able to return to who I am today. The study and practice of yoga philosophy allowed me to zoom out and find "sama darshana", or equal vision, and "sama vritti" that is even mind. I realized that happiness does not depend on what is happening outside, it's an internal experience.

In writing this book, I only hope some of my experiences can benefit others and help them navigate to uncomplicate the dynamics of working in a corporate environment. This book humbly gives advice, not only from my experience and observations, but also from some of the incredible mentors and friends whom I am grateful for. My philosophy is based on a strong and undeniable foundation of ancient yogic texts, which had a profound impact in all aspects of my life and others. Today I work as an internationally licensed yoga therapist, a life coach, and a yoga and meditation teacher both in corporate settings and with individuals. Yoga philosophy has been an invaluable guide for my professional and personal life.

As I continue to explore and study yoga, it is for certain that my perspective and articulation of subjects will certainly grow and shift. Nothing is permanent in this material realm. Therefore, it's hard to put contexts in definitive manner. I humbly remind the reader to have discernment and take what they feel is useful in promoting their well-being.

As much as we'd like to think we are far superior to previous generations, our basic human nature has not changed. Everything we invent serves to make our lives faster and supposedly easier, but at times, it seems to only complicate it further. This book hopes to be a guide to uncomplicate some of these at the workplace.

What is this human journey all about? Once you pause and start questioning, then it's possible to find real answers. *So, this book is for those who question...*

CHAPTER 1

FORGET SAFETY

You are born from the children of God's creation,
but you have fixed your sight too low.
How can you be happy?
Come, return to the root of the root of your Self.
~ Rumi

Starting something new or having to make a choice is never easy. Especially when it comes to choosing a job. It may be overwhelming to having to decide "what is the best path for me" followed by, "what if I make a mistake".

It is in our nature to seek comfort and run away from a challenge. We think by placing ourselves in situations where "we think" we can control, we avoid pain. We forget the very situation which starts easy can lead to difficulty. Comfort seduces us with an illusion of safety, but it hinders our growth. Embracing discomfort is what allows us to grow and

1

be in the rhythm of everything in the universe. This makes life more purposeful and joyful, as we meet challenges and overcome them; we find satisfaction in action.

In the early 2000's I took a job because it seemed easy and did not ask a lot of me and it gave me financial stability. I did not feel fulfilled in the job (I was a VP for a Transfer Company) but I kept at it because it gave me the time and freedom to do what I really wanted, self-exploration. It allowed me to take the courses I needed. Some of which were trainings in coaching and psychology. But like anything in life, when you do things for selfish reasons, you are not doing anyone any favors including yourself. It's ok to pause and reflect – but doing a job that never was yours, this simply does not bring happiness. After two years I found myself looking for a job that satisfied my soul. With that mindset, I found an opportunity where I had to use everything I learned professionally and personally up to that point, to re-structure an organization. I realized, there would be a time when I could do what I truly love, until then, the solution was not to downgrade, instead, to reach for an opportunity that would help me apply what I learned and help me to grow.

When it comes to searching for a job, "comfort" may not be what you want, or on top of your wish list. Discomfort is necessary for growth, as it signals ego is at work, trying to hold on to the status quo. But like all aspects of life, nothing is stagnant, everything is moving and changing like our own bodies. From childhood to adult, to an older age. The word "path" implies movement in a certain direction. Therefore, there are two aspects of it. Movement and directionality.

Without moving, there is no way to figure out the right direction just from contemplation.

Moving for the sake of moving is not what I am getting at. Certainly, there needs to be reflection and cultivation of self-awareness.

How do you know it's the right job for you?

1. Practicality check:
   - It meets your monetary needs
   - It utilizes your talents
   - It fits the lifestyle you choose. (i.e., Timing/location/ work-life balance, culture, and environment)
2. Feeling check:
   - It excites you
   - It scares you
   - It makes you question yourself (am I capable of doing this?)
   - It inspires you
   - It gives you hope and aspiration. (You believe you have the potential to grow in it)
3. Purpose check:
   - The ideals of the company align with yours
   - The job you are taking is a step towards your vision of your future self.

Remember! Don't choose a job:

* For money
* Because it's easy
* You don't like

Right now, you might find yourself in a job that is not your dream job, but an easy or convenient one. And if so, don't beat yourself up about it, but understand exactly what it is and begin the process of finding something better or more aligned with your passion.

One of my clients determined, through our sessions, she would love to work for "The" Social Media Company, but she felt she did not have the right skill set and she would not be enough as she came from the Banking Industry. Although she had identified her dream company, she did not believe in herself. However, during our sessions, by recognizing and slowly releasing her negative beliefs and perspective, she started seeing her strengths and how she could be an asset to that company. She was highly intelligent and realized the very thing she was holding onto (status quo!) was making her unhappy. She was ready to get out of her comfort zone and all she needed was a gentle nudge and a support system to allow her to move forward. She ended up getting a job at her dream company, but it was not easy at the beginning. After a year of struggle with many ups and downs, she received a promotion, and full confidence in herself.

How you start a job determines its future. Often, when a job begins with difficulty, it eventually become easier and gratifying. This does not mean the job gets any easier; it means you grew and developed to meet the challenges.

The lesson is to embrace fear, insecurity and doubt.**" What scares you may be blessing you as in darkness only can we see the light."

Procrastination

Procrastination can show up when you are looking for a job at the beginning of your career. Many recent college graduates I work with, show this symptom of procrastination when it comes time to apply for jobs. Or when you feel stuck in a job and know you need to make a change, but somehow can't seem to get around to it. Or even at your day-to-day life.

At some point I am sure you also put off doing something that needs to be done. Maybe you overbooked yourself – "did not have the time", or you did not have the self-confidence, or even hoped by avoiding it you could avoid dealing with uncomfortable emotions such as fear of failure.

The truth is you will have uncomfortable situations, you will experience failure as well as success as it's the condition of this universe; Duality exists all around us. Warm sun and cool moon, winter and summer seasons, day and night. But like in all these examples, these are all temporary conditions. Similarly, you will experience situations/people/jobs that you like, and you don't like.

Basak Gunaydin

If you do things based on preferences; this means you will also miss a big chunk of your life with endless possibilities.

One of my friends who has recently retired from a very successful career in Banking Law and Investment Industries, revealed to me that one of the keys to his success was to never procrastinate. Being decisive and moving forward with conviction was a key element to his leadership.

Essentially procrastination has to do with not having resilience. Resilience is the capacity to adopt to any adversity, or challenge which is ongoing. When you don't have the coping skills for the emotions and reactions the situation would bring up, you will procrastinate.

When I work with my clients, I emphasize building resilience before they start a new job search or do a career change

How to build resilience:

1. Down regulate the SNS (sympathetic nervous system): Learn to relax through meditation, alone time, digital detox, joyful activities and hobbies, travel
2. Developing physical fitness: Choose a practice that you enjoy and do it! Whether it's yoga or cycling, do it continuously, in a safe way. A strong body equals a strong mind.
3. Practice awareness: Utilize meditation and breath practices
4. Zoom out: Focus on the big picture
5. Connect with your community: Surrounding yourself with like-minded people will help motivate you.

Having a healthy support system which you can reach when you need help is invaluable.

6. Laugh more: Joyful attitude in life will help relieve the unnecessary stress we put on ourselves.

Awareness Meditation with Body Scan

Take a comfortable seat. Close your eyes. Become aware of the room you are in.

Notice the sounds in the space. Temperature of the room. Any smell, any taste in the mouth. Now bring your awareness to your body. Toes to heel relax the right foot. Let the left foot be steady. Move your awareness to the right leg. Ankle, to calf, to knee and thigh. Right leg is motionless. Left leg, ankle to knee to hip, immovable. Take the awareness to the pelvic floor; front of the pelvis, glutes, low back; relax. Let the muscles of the whole back relax. Bring the awareness to the right hand. Fingertips to wrist; still. Left hand is steady. Right arm: wrist to elbow to shoulder; stable. Left arm, relax. Back of the neck is solid; head is completely still. Take the awareness to the whole body and release the tension in the whole body. As body relaxes more move the awareness to the breath, at the entrance of the nostrils. Try not to control it; just simply observe. Notice the slight temperature change; incoming breath is slightly cooler, outgoing breath is slightly warmer. Keep your attention on your breath. Let the thoughts enter the mind in and out without engaging in them, bring your awareness back to your breath.

CHAPTER 2

INTER-VIEW

Don't go away, come near.
Don't be faithless, be faithful.
Find the antidote in the venom.
Come to the root of the root of yourself
~ Rumi

There is a lot written about how to interview for a job. But if you pause and look, the word itself gives us a hint as to what an interview is all about. "Inter" as a prefix means between or reciprocal, plus "Inter" implies interior or inner. Therefore, one can think of the word as a combination of the two. Inter-View: Sharing a view of your inner self.

For many people, an interview has become indicative of a scary and intense experience, but if it is reinterpreted as an exchange for both parties involved, the fear dissipates. An interview is simply a time in which you allow someone to see who you are. Since there's no directionality to the word, it's an exchange for both parties involved.

I have conducted thousands of interviews during my career. As I gained knowledge and experience, my interview skills became more refined. Here's what it all boils down to: show me who you are so I can release my biases and see *you;* not your resume, not your accomplishments and education, but the true you. In that exchange of seeing and being seen, the interview happens.

Considering the emotional charge of the situation, the interviewer must set the tone and create a space for the interviewee to be clear, open and honest.

How to be a good Interviewer:

At the beginning of my career, I did not look forward to interviewing people because I was in a rush to fill a position by trying to fit an individual into a job function. In time I learned this was not the best approach. Instead, I realized hiring good people who are not only qualified but also enthusiastic and interesting (so they make the job function *function* for them), is the recipe for success. As a result, I began seeing the person, not the resume.

Perhaps you have been in interviews where the interviewer has not met your gaze because they are too busy looking at your resume or they are only focused on seeing if you "fit." Throughout my career I learned from experienced managers, both what to do and what not to do, and eventually I developed my own interview style. I learned to ask questions that will tell me what is untold, what lies beneath the presentation allowing the interviewee to relax and speak freely and share their personality and values. Because of this, many times I decided within minutes of meeting a candidate they were right for the job.

Some of these questions were:

- What in the job description interests you?
- What are your hobbies?
- What was your favorite job through your career and why? And least favorite one, as a follow up
- What is most important to you in your job? (i.e., Company/people I work with/ office set up/ benefits/ type of projects etc.)

If anything, an interview is an opportunity to get into someone else's world, to learn about their experiences and how they may be of value to your organization. You never want to hire someone who will continue doing the job as it was. You should want a person who shines a new light on the position and therefore will advance the job and themselves. Good companies want their people to grow so they, themselves simultaneously continue to grow. At the same time, it's your job to put forth a realistic overview and expectations of the job – as you do not want to work with someone who will be unhappy all the time.

When I interviewed S for a job it was clear she did not have the experience and her background did not fit the requirements of the job, but she had the education and talent. What made me decide to hire her was her! She was enthusiastic, interested and asked me great questions. She was honest and she knew she could meet the challenge with genuine interest. She was confident and straight forward, did not hide herself. So, I was able to "see" her. It was a gamble to hire her. My superiors questioned my decision. But I believed in her and wanted her to succeed. And did she succeed! She very quickly became extremely good at her job and brought new ideas and different perspectives. This is one of many examples I witnessed over time.

Interviewee

If you are the interviewee, the most important aspect of the exchange is to bring your most authentic self to the interview. If you are hungry, sleep deprived, or tired you cannot possibly be presenting yourself in the best light. Having a certain amount of anxiety is natural. There are ways to calm the nerves and the mind. Sometimes wanting the job so much can create more anxiety. The antidote is to trust that regardless of outcome, this situation is designed to lead you on the path you are meant for. This does not mean not to do your best, on the contrary, you must put the effort in but try not to be attached to the results. Also, and this is important; try not to fit yourself into the job but think of what you can bring to the role.

Visualization practices can be very helpful. Imagine yourself speaking to the interviewer, telling them why you are a great candidate for this job. See yourself having already got the job, imagine yourself in the office environment. This way you are sending subliminal messages that you are the right person for the job.

Here are some tips:

Before the interview...

Practical:

- Do your research – Know the company and what it stands for.
- Bring a copy of your resume and other presentation materials – in case they did not print them out or others are called into the interview.
- Be early and/or call-in advance in case of an unforeseen delay.
- Try not to re-schedule the interview unless it's absolutely necessary.
- Present your best self (sleep well, clean up, dress up, etc.).
- Don't eat a few hours before – so you are not sluggish and your mind is alert and not engaged in physical activity, like digestion/elimination.

Emotional:

- Meditate or at least take some deep breaths a few minutes before – to calm the mind and relax the body.
- Get out of your own way – stop listening to the negative self-talk.

- Create an affirmation, a mantra, for your interview, such as "I am enough" "I shine through" "I am relaxed" "I am open" "I make a great impression".
- Prepare as if you got the job already. Visualize yourself having the job and see yourself in that environment as often as possible.

During the interview...

- Be your authentic self.
- Get out of your own way; Remember to breathe, so you are not in the mind but in your body and are present.
- Listen more speak less * See more about active listening, in chapter 5.
- Connect to your interviewer(s) observe them in an effort to get to know them without judgement. They will become your reflection, as you see them in a positive light, in turn they start seeing you the same way which is called Projecting self-image.
- Answer their questions, don't stay on your agenda or say what you prepared to say. Keep your energy high. No one wants to hire someone with no enthusiasm and energy. But too much of that is not appropriate either so try not to drink too much coffee before the interview.
- Be polite and express gratitude for the person's time and attention, even if they are in a foul mood. Consider you don't know what their day has been like, what stresses they maybe under.

- Be prepared with 2 or 3 questions about the company in case you are given space to ask: Some examples are:

  1. Specifications and expectations for the job you are applying for.
  2. Company goals, history and future, culture.
  3. About the interviewer and their experience.
  4. About your direct manager how he/she is known and their management style.

After the interview...

- Send a note of appreciation to the interviewer for their time and contribution
- Express precisely why you are the best candidate for the job (If you want the job)
- Follow up if you don't hear back either way, within a week
- Make a note of highlights and maybe some low lights if there were, as learning tool

One of my clients who owns a Law Firm mentioned that once in an interview her interviewee spoke for an hour and a half straight. She could say only three sentences the whole time. She said she was exhausted and thinks of it as one of the worst interviews she did. She said her best interviews are when a person exudes passion talking about their past experiences and humble about their achievements.

The golden key to be a great interviewer or to give a good interview is the ability to connect with others. I am talking about an authentic connection, here. This is only possible when you can have an authentic connection with yourself. So, stop hiding or showing a different you, start finding out who you are, what makes you, YOU! This is your best asset!

4-Part Breathing Practice for Balanced Mind

Sit comfortably and close your eyes. Bring the whole body into stillness. Notice your breath at the entrance of the nostrils. Try not to control but observe it. Notice 4 parts of the breath; Inhalation, followed by a split second of retention on the top of the inhale. Then exhalation with a split second of retention at the bottom of the exhale. Keep your mind in these 4 parts.

Now equalizing the 4 parts; start inhaling in 4 counts then hold the breath for 4 counts, exhale for 4 counts and hold the breath for 4 counts. If it's too hard, move down to 3; too easy, move up to 5. Try not to have any exertion on your breath. After several rounds, return the breath to normal and slowly open your eyes.

CHAPTER 3

OBSERVING THE BATTLEFIELD:
FIRST WEEKS AT THE OFFICE

"Don't be satisfied with stories,
how things have gone with others.
Unfold your own myth."
~ Rumi

Your first weeks in a new company is a golden opportunity, not to be wasted. This is the time to see objectively, all the workings of the organization. The time to set up for your whole journey. You shouldn't jump in too quickly nor sit back too long as you miss valuable opportunities. Consider the workplace as a battlefield, which a warrior (you) must be prepared to enter.

The analogy of the workplace, as a battlefield is not new. Adidas employees, in their Portland offices labeled their meeting rooms as "war rooms". Political campaigns often call their strategy hot spots "war rooms." When there's work to be done and many people involved, there will be oppositions, confrontations, even hostility. How do you prepare yourself for this?

In the Bhagavat Gita, one of the most prominent texts in Yoga,* Kurukshetra, where the war is taking place, is described as a warplane but also a holly land that pilgrims visit. Pilgrimage means to take a journey to a place or to a higher consciousness, closer to the divine. In the same way, a workplace may be viewed as a battlefield which also, can become a place of worship. Conflicts and shift in dynamics, when approached as an opportunity, can create transformation. To be clear, any amount of transformation and growth in life, comes from a challenge, otherwise there would be no need for a change. So, expect and be ready for the challenges. Change starts from an individual level. By shifting your perspective, you can change your experience. what we experience in life comes from our consciousness. When we understand this, instead of trying to point fingers at others or to change other's opinions, we look at ourselves to understand how we had a hand in creating the situation we are in. In this way we can also start taking steps towards more beneficial outcome.

You have a huge opportunity in the first weeks at a new job to observe from a detached point of view not yet sullied by your own agenda. You can then contemplate how you may be of service, what gifts and talents would be most useful and what might hinder your potential for growth and success.

Here are some tips to guide you in the first weeks in a new job:

Do:

1. Observe: Your first day at the job is to survey the workplace to understand not just your job but also others; to digest the dynamics, the mechanics, the various relationships. This is the most precious time before you are in it and too close to it. You have the vantage point, you can see what is working and what is not, objectively.

2. Ask then Listen: If you are in a leadership position, you must hear the people who are reporting to you with an open mind and with "active listening", so you hear what is beyond the surface and the stories told. Active listening means having discernment, to watch out for the distinction between the facts and the gossip. Most of the time we get too close to a story, and we forget the origin of it. This is why observation is the key. Most successful people understand the value of observation from a detached perspective.

    *   Ask what's working: So you don't try to reinvent the wheel and focus on the wrong things. Also asking someone what's working the best is to give a gift, as it gets them in touch with the values and gifts they get from their job. Most of the time we are focused on all the things that don't work in our lives. Gratitude changes one's attitude and

Basak Gunaydin

        as an extension, one's experience. Also, it gives you an insight on the person you are speaking to.

* Ask for what's not working: Now this is why you are hired. Find out from different people what seems to be challenging operationally, process wise and communication channels.

* Ask your manager what the expectations/milestones/targets are so you and they are very clear about what you need to deliver and when. This will be one of the keys to your measurement of success later on.

3. Create your own Philosophy: You are the controller of your own experience at the workplace. You the leader of your domain. Those who are influenced by other's ideas and opinions will not understand this but to establish your base, you need to form your own opinions. We are not all having the same experiences in life, our attitude changes our worldview and our philosophy through the stories we tell ourselves... These narratives shape our experience. Therefore, it's important that you design a narrative that inspires you, puts you into action, not one that degrades you and lets you down from the get-go. For example, if you listen to someone complaining about how they are not receiving the recognition they deserve and how no one is being supportive and so on, this will trick your mind into thinking this is the norm, making their experience your experience. In doing so, you may start giving up and not caring about your

tasks, and in this way you will not get recognition or support as well.

If you do not buy into the idea of this persons' own negative experience as an ultimate truth, you don't allow it to cloud your perspective and impact your functions. You will then have your own unique experience.

4. Form alliances: There is immense power in forming alliances, creating your associations for the common cause. Achievements require group effort at the workplace. To find like-minded individuals empowers you and your causes.

Don't:

1. Get caught up in gossip: Try and hear the truth within the gossip, it's a waste of time to pay attention to drama, which is often very attractive. Sometimes a little bit of it is necessary to form connections. But don't overdo it especially at the beginning.

2. Speak too soon: Don't jump and voice an opinion the first day at work unless you are asked to. You are more likely to be heard after you understand the company and have assessed the situation at hand.

3. Assume you know: Every situation is a learning opportunity. Even if you came from a similar job at another company, every company does things differently. Stay humble

4. Spend too much time on your phone/checking social media (unless your job requires it).

First impressions are important, most people draw their conclusions within seconds of meeting you. Some of these you cannot help as they have to do with their own belief systems and stories they tell themselves. You can keep your emotions and reactions in check and respond to situations from a well informed and thoughtful place. This requires of course, having your own intentions and your belief systems in check.

If in the first few weeks in a new job maintain a humble attitude, applying some restraint and detachment, practicing active listening, and observing skills, you can shape both your experience and that of your colleagues, as well.

Practice for Improving Observation Skills

Choose a yoga pose to hold for a few minutes, i.e., plank. Notice the sensations in the body. Become aware of the feelings and thoughts which arise in the mind due to these sensations. Now stay with the pose and bring your focus to the parts of the body that are having difficulty. Then direct your breath to these parts and start extending and deepening your breath. Can you bring some spaciousness within the thoughts and feelings? Try not to get involved in the mind-chatter, simply observe your breath and notice if there is any information, or inner wisdom that arise from it.

---

4 TYPES OF PEOPLE AND
3 MODES OF NATURE

Once you get hold of selflessness,
You'll be dragged from your ego
and freed from many traps.
Come, return to the root of the root of your Self

Everyone has their own personality and ego which is built by years of experiences. It's necessary to have a healthy dose of ego because it helps to get things done, puts you on your path. But if one starts identifying with one's ego too closely, thinking only in terms of "me and mine" there's a danger of having a false ego. False ego is one who thinks "I am the doer, the world revolves around me, and/or the world owes me... etc." A False ego traps you in isolation, inflexibility and as a result, loneliness.

At the workplace it's important to identify the different personalities you are dealing with and have the ability to get out of your skin and relate to other's.

I had a situation at work with one of the people in my department. This person was not performing well, their communication was not effective. Almost everyone including my boss wanted them to be gone. I was not so sure. I knew more about them than most people did. Objectively, I could see where the problem lay. It was not the person but the job and environment. I was really unsure of how to resolve this situation. Should I let this person go? I had hired and fired many people, but each time I was convinced of my actions. This time was different, I could see the value of the person. So, I went to my yoga teacher and asked him what I should do. He said words I have never forgotten from that moment on; "Jobs come and go, you always put the people first!" This situation required me to rise, to be flexible and be creative. So, I did. Rather than trying to fit the person into the job, I revised the job to best utilize their talents. In the end this strategy served this person and the company. I am friends with them to this day as they realized that I stood up for them.

Always put people and relationships ahead of the work that needs to get done/ a deal that must be signed/ a sale that must be accomplished.

However, if you are always putting people first, you need to be an expert in people. The following is one way – a way outlined by the Bhagavad Gita thousands of years ago that will help you deal with every person in every situation.

FOUR TYPES OF PEOPLE

There are 4 types of people you will meet in the workplace or in life, in general... Sometimes the same person will exhibit all four of these characteristics based on time and circumstance.

1. Good People
2. Difficult or wicked people
3. Lucky people
4. Unlucky (sufferers) people

GOOD PEOPLE

This is the category of people with good intentions, knowledge seekers. It's easy to be friendly toward the people who just want to do their job, who want to do it the best way possible, to learn and grow. These people look for opportunities to help others, encourage others and become reliable and trustworthy in the workplace. Therefore, appreciate and befriend those who work not just to their benefit but for the greater good.

WICKED PEOPLE

It's much harder to work with people who are either difficult or even harmful; those who do everything for their own benefit, to climb the corporate ladder at the expense of others, to take all the credit, to control, to overpower. But the art of knowing is *knowing what to ignore*. If all you think about is "how wrong and difficult this person is", you are engaging with them in a way that is not healthy; not for you or them. The best way of dealing with this type of person is to not engage with them, try not to judge and keep a healthy distance. But sometimes this is easier said than done! For example, if this person is your boss, best way to interact with them would be to see what is good about them and appreciate those qualities and learn from their mistakes – without judging them and taking it personally. Know that everyone is dealing with their own karmic* baggage. Do not get into confrontations and challenge them. Do the job to the best of your ability and don't get hung up on their impressions of you.

LUCKY PEOPLE

Then there's those lucky people! Those who get things easier than others, who always land on their feet. Envy is the most dangerous human emotion as it eats you away and lets you forget your own individuality, your own gifts. Being happy for these people allows you to appreciate their qualities and learn to harness your own.

UNLUCKY PEOPLE

The unlucky people are those who always complain about everything. They look for something wrong in any situation and make that the center of their experience. It's easy to dismiss them quickly and not engage with them. But since these types of people are hurting themselves and influencing the moral of the company, the best approach would be to have understanding and compassion and let them feel they are heard – include them in creating solutions.

Everyone is under the influence of three modes of nature. These are subtle forces, called gunas* that influence our behavior as well as all aspects of our physical, mental and emotional being.

Modes of Nature

1. Goodness (Sattva)
2. Passion (Rajas)
3. Ignorance, Dullness, Laziness (Tamas)

These three modes show up everywhere around us. For example.

In nature: Spring and Fall are in the mode of goodness. Winter in the mode of dullness, Summer with its heat in passion.

In the Ocean you can see all three modes. The surface may be in the mode of passion with its wavy texture. The middle part in goodness, calm and beautifu,l and the bottom part of the ocean in dullness.

In food: Spicy foods are in the mode of passion, foods that are rich in carbs like pasta and sugar, in the mode of dullness, making us feel heavy and lethargic, green vegetables, fruits in the mode of goodness.

In our day: mornings are sattvic, mid-day rajasic, evenings, tamasic

In the workplace: You will meet people who speak fast and are quick to anger; who are acting out of passion or those who are disinterested, slow to react, maybe a little sleepy; who are acting out of dullness. Then those who bring the best out in everyone, who are calm and good natured, who are acting out of goodness. You can see all these qualities in the same person at different times, even in the same day.

We can go on; I think you got the point. You can see these changing moods in yourself and everyone around you.

As you understand this, you realize everyone is acting out of the influence of these modes or moods. In this way rather than taking things personally, you can respond thoughtfully. The key is understanding and seeing that when someone is in passion or ignorance modes, it's a passing moment. It can easily be replaced by goodness. Our true nature yearns to be seen and understood. Through patience, open heart and mind we can cultivate more goodness in ourselves and in others. In this way we can create a healthy environment.

If we look through the lens of material modes of nature, we can see someone we consider as "good people" are generally in the mode of goodness, same as the "lucky people". Difficult people are most likely in the mode of passion and unlucky people, in the mode of dullness. But the modes of nature do not determine what the potential of the people are. The key is to interact with others not from their imbalance these modes create, but from their true nature. This requires an understanding that with all the differences we may have and unique talents and gifts as individuals, labels and assumed roles, there is a fundamental quality within each and every one of us which is joyful, full of knowledge and bliss.

While working as a VP of Design for a previous company, the new CFO, who came from Wall Street, would greet me with a head-to toe look (you know the look!) as I enter the boardroom for a meeting and comment on "how I look" then ask me to "smile more". In an all men boardroom being singled out and put in a "woman box" like that was the most humiliating thing, which I know some of the readers can very much relate to! One might call it bullying. As difficult and stressful as it was to be subjected to that, I also understood it did not necessarily mean this person was "bad or difficult" it meant he was in effect in a mode of nature, which we call Tamas, or ignorance, to other's situation and the environment he was creating. In this way, I was able to respond to him and pointed out his behavior from a place of assertiveness and confidence without allowing myself to conform or become angry.

Loving Kindness Meditation

1. Bring a person in your mind who you like/love. Visualize as if they are sitting across from you. Looking deeply in their eyes notice the feelings and sensations arise in your mind and body by thinking of this person. Mentally say these to this person.

   "May you be happy
   May you be healthy
   May you be filled with peace
   May you feel love in your heart"

2. Now let this person go and this time pick someone who you are neutral about maybe the person you see every morning in the train station, a neighbor, delivery guy, etc.
   Repeat the same phrases for this person as you visualize them in front of you.

3. This time bring a person who you dislike, who is stressing you. Offer these phrases to this person.

4. Finally bring your awareness in your heart space and direct these phrases to yourself

CHAPTER 5

COMMUNICATION IS EVERYTHING

Half of Life is lost in charming others
Other half, going through anxieties caused by others
Leave this play, you played enough
~ Rumi

Communication means sending and receiving information, it's a two-way street (like through phone lines or computers). When you ask for information on your search engine, you want a simple clear response. You want the same when you communicate at the workplace. Though, in many instances, communication is misunderstood as "venting", "complaining", "blaming".

People complain a lot about "not being heard" or "not being understood", but whose responsibility is it to be heard or understood? It's yours alone. Like everything, this requires some attention and training. The lower mind is constantly in the mode of either fighting, defending, or disappearing. It takes a higher intelligence to pause and evaluate what to say or how to respond. Your words can dramatically shift the direction of a topic.

Words are powerful, they open a window to one's mind. Your expression is everything. Your words create a reality, and you want that reality to be an expression of your truth. It is your responsibility to communicate authentically.

A thoughtful communication requires:

1. Active listening
2. Having an intention
3. A humble attitude

1. Active Listening

#1 rule of communication is *Listening*. This applies not only in a professional environment but in every type of relationship in life. The function of "hearing" is not merely a physiological function done through ears, passively. Active listening requires the engagement of all your facilities, the body, mind and intellect. We instinctively engage some of these but paying attention to the three will make us more effective communicators.

We all have selective hearing. If there are ten people in the room, there will be ten different stories told about what is heard. So listening is not only a function of hearing.

According to the teachings of yoga, our bodies are made up of five energetic layers or sheaths, called koshas*, imagine the Russian nesting dolls.

The physical body, including our senses, the subtle body which is comprised of life force energy (breath or prana), mind and intellect, and the causal body which is our most inner self. Active listening requires an engagement of all these layers.

How does this work? Let me explain from the outermost to the inner layer.

- Physical – Listening through senses such as sight and hearing. Body language gives away more information than the words spoken. Nonverbal gestures and movements can express information; such as facial expressions, body postures, gestures, touch and use of space.
- Energetic – While you are hearing someone, you also "feel" their energy. Sometimes this energy aspect of their being tells you more than what is being said. When someone is speaking with high energy and enthusiasm, we become more engaged. If a person is exuding confidence, we want to trust them, or if someone is being arrogant in their delivery, we immediately question or judge them. These energetic cues help guide the conversation consciously or unconsciously.
- Mind – Mind functions based on likes and dislikes are rooted in previous experiences, it's like a

database. The mind is also very fast, makes very quick decisions based on preferences and is focused on defending (the false ego). When someone is speaking you get access to how their mind works. Where do they focus, what is important to them, what are their values and triggers?

Their breathing pattern is a big clue as well as it is connected to their mind. If one is speaking fast, you know they are not breathing deeply, and shallow breath is an indicator they are speaking from their lower mind, either defending or fighting. If someone starts breathing slowly and deeply you know they are considering or contemplating not just via the mind but from a slightly removed, higher point of view.

- Intelligence – Intelligence is the discriminating factor. Intelligence fixed in knowledge responds to situations strategically, introducing new perspectives, tailoring our presentation to other's listening. Slow deep breath is an indicator that a person is present, and their higher intelligence is involved as they use their time to engage all their facilities to come up with creative solutions.

- Spiritual – This is where a person's philosophy lives. Everyone has their own philosophy, their own perspective. This spiritual dimension enables individuals to create, discover and apply meaning, purpose and values in their life's situations. Understanding a person's perspective is a key in how to communicate with them and engage them in the workplace. Most companies make a big mistake in this aspect. They try to enforce the values of a few leaders in the large group rather than trying to understand the values of the larger demographic and inspire them through their shared values.

Therefore, to actively listen, you must engage your senses, pay attention to your breath, and notice what is pulling the mind away and creating emotion. Intelligence works slower than the mind. The mind is very sharp and quick to react, while it takes more time for intelligence to kick in as it has a voyage to make through the physical, emotional, and energetic dimensions. By noticing all these aspects of yourself and in others, you are engaging your higher faculties so you can hear not only what is being said but also what is not said – and tailor your response to the person who is listening, and in this way become a more intelligent communicator.

2. Having an Intention

Once you know your audience, through active listening, you have the advantage of shaping your communication to their listening. Effective communication depends on intention. Your messaging must convey your intention. When you have a clear, holistic, and powerful intention, then expression is much easier as you take your ego out of the equation. In other words, you are no longer the subject but the deliverer of the message. Intentionality also combats the attachment. When you are not attached to having a specific outcome but committed to your intention, then you open yourself up to feedback and a real discussion. In that way you invite the others to participate and engage with the subject.

It's important to take a moment to evaluate your intention in the dialogue. To check in with yourself as to whether what you are saying is coming from your false ego as a reaction or is what you are about to say contributing to the conversation, creating an action toward a beneficial result for all parties.

3. Humble Attitude

We see the world according to (our own) the lenses we look through. Our attitude shapes our experience. Therefore, your attitude is very important. I can't stress enough the importance of having a humble attitude. Whether you are a manager or an employee, you assume a position of a leader in the work you do. A humble leader acknowledging what he/she does not know, is more approachable, forgiving, motivating and inviting.

A humble attitude in communication, will open the channels for others to interact freely, share ideas and ultimately will expand the scope of the discussion. Pride and ego will take away from your intention.

Effective communication is about listening, understanding, adopting, clarity and intention. In this, you need to take responsibility for your communication and ask yourself if what you are about to say is helpful or necessary in what you are communicating – and be kind. If the conversation or presentation did not go the way you planned because you were not in the right frame of mind, then there's always an opportunity to follow up, own your mistakes and revisit the situation.

Difficult people and how to deal with them

Be careful about whoever comes, because
Each has been sent as a guide, from beyond
~ Rumi

Everyone has a person at work they can't stand. It's just nature. We are in constant duality, likes and dislikes. These are the people you learn the most from, you learn how not to be, or you learn to adjust similar qualities in yourself.

Here are the keys to dealing with difficult people:

1. Do not Reject them: Most of the time people who seem difficult are those who are dealing with their own emotions, sometimes too publicly. Their foremost desire is usually, to be seen. So, by giving time and attention to them you will make them feel valued and heard.

2. Be Curious: Rather than judging them, be curious about what is motivating them to act a certain way. Knowledge is power. Once you understand the core of the issue, you can find solutions.

3. Inquire within: Usually people who irk you are triggering a part of you that you reject or label as "bad". It's never a coincidence that you meet such people in your life, as it forces you to face and heal parts of your own psyche. As you make peace with

these parts of yourself, you can transform your relationship to these people

4. Be Compassionate: Unless you are able to put yourself in someone else's shoes, and be empathetic, it's hard to find compassion for these people. But compassion starts from within. This is an opportunity to look within yourself; where are you being hard and unforgiving towards yourself?

One of my friends, who worked as a high-level executive, in prominent and well-known Designer Brands through her career shared with me about a person she worked with in one of these companies, who was equal to her in terms of his title and responsibilities in an area that required a partnership with her. She described this person as ego centric, wanting credit for everything. This person told their international manufacturing partners during his travels that they should not listen to her but only him. Once she heard this, upon his return, she asked for a meeting with him and discussed the situation openly and told him she would not put up with it. She insisted they have an open and honest communication and do what is right for the company. She assured him what she wanted was a healthy, productive partnership.

See, she could easily avoid this discussion, even reciprocate what he did to her. But what would that do. Avoiding or fighting back only makes matters worse, taking her attention from work, cloud her judgement, creating unnecessary stress (which will eventually affect the whole environment) and maybe even quit the job to not to deal with the situation.

But every time you walk away from a difficult person or a situation, you are not punishing them but yourself as when you don't overcome these situations, you are creating more bondage and not freeing yourself from them. She stood for herself and for him and in the end created a harmonious, supportive and respectful working relationship. She told me she stayed friendly with this person to this date, years after having this situation.

The Art of Arguing

> *"He who knows only his own side of the*
> *case knows little of that."*
> ~ *John Stuart Mill*

Arguing is an art and it needs to be evaluated as an art. To be good at it, one needs to study and practice to understand the craft. Otherwise, you can easily make it about you and not the subject at hand. Our points of view are often too polarized, and this shows up as people hearing only the view with which they already agree and dismissing the opposing views. Then either attacking, defending or just avoiding the conversation as to avoid confrontation. There needs to be flexibility and openness to hear a different point of view and be able to pause and go "aww that's a great point!"

Most of the time when we argue with someone with an opposing or alternative view, what we are doing has nothing to do with the subject itself. The exchange becomes emotionally charged and each person becomes focused on justifying their own strongly held beliefs, which are often based on their attachments.

Here are some key points to the art of arguing:

DO:

- Listen: I know I am repeating myself here, but it bears repeating…it's the most important factor, knowing what you are arguing against. So many times, people argue when in fact, they have the exact same point of view, which they may be expressing differently. This only serves to waste time and energy.

- Understand the opposing view: Quoting Stephen Covey: "Seek first to understand, then be understood". Until you are able to fully understand the opposing view as if it were your own, you are not able to defend yours intelligently

- Repeat the opposing view: Once you have understood the opposing view, then retell the view without leaving anything out so the opposing party has a chance to "hear" it. They might be surprised. Because sometimes we are not fully aware of what we are saying. The mind is making decisions (agree/disagree/attack/defend/ avoid) so fast, that we can't catch up to it. Hearing one's argument out loud allows one to see the point of view they have and sometimes in that, they dismantle it. Also being understood gives us the impression of value (since we are mostly looking for acknowledgement at the workplace) that allows the emotions to calm down.

When one listens to you then they hear what they said and catch themselves as mostly they are unaware of what they are asking.

- Speak the Facts. Rather than getting into the story, which than creates more story, stick to the facts and present solutions

- Make it impersonal: This is the hardest aspect. Keep the discussion in a professional place even if the other party does not. Don't get hooked into drama. Remember the higher purpose.

- Breathe: When you are not breathing, you are in the automatic mode in the lower brain. Paying attention to the breath calms the mind and allows the intelligence to be present.

- Stick to your intention: Don't just argue to argue, to be right or to overpower etc. (Whatever your lower self is getting out of it). Keep your intention at the forefront. What am I trying to get out of this discussion?

Asking for what you want

Asking for something is generally difficult, so most people wait to get acknowledgement from higher ups. But this a passive, wishful approach which does not always work. I have coached many people on how to ask for a raise, advancement in their role/title, for part time work, or work from home situations, just to list a few. In the raise situation, most managers do not want to upset the budget of their department. If you are directly speaking with the CEO or

CFO of the company, they would rather wait until being asked to put more money forward. We associate our worth with what we get paid, but this is rarely the case. …

Asking for part time or a day off from work is another difficult task. No one likes to change, and this includes your managers. So how do you go about it? Here are a few tips.

- Prepare for the meeting:

This may sound obvious, but many people don't put in as much preparation as it requires for something so important for themselves as much as they do for a business meeting or presentation.

1. Physically: Write down first your accomplishments, your projects and tasks don't assume they know or remember everything. Especially if you need to speak to someone who is not day to day with you. This is also for you to see what you do. It's your resume. Promote yourself. Then write how would what you are asking for, benefit the company. **(very important)

2. Mentally: Check your beliefs and doubts. If you don't believe in it yourself, how do you expect others to believe in you? If you are hesitant or afraid, notice what is in the way of you expressing your needs. Be fully convinced, you deserve what you are asking for.

3. Emotionally: It's okay to show emotion during your conversation but it needs to be controlled and not over the top, so it works to your benefit. Reviewing

what types of emotions comes up for you before the meeting helps. Running your request by a trusted advisor is very beneficial.

4. Energetically: Everything is a vibration of energy. Send energy to the conversation, days before. Prior to your meeting visualize you have already received what you are asking for, and keep speaking to your manager, before you speak to them. They will receive the message subliminally, so when you have the actual conversation, it's not a new one for them. You can do this (in advance) as many times, and as long as you wish.

• When you are in the meeting:

DO:

• Keep your Energy high: You want to be enthusiastic, not depressed.
• Keep a good posture: good posture exudes confidence.
• Express gratitude: No one will give you anything if you make them feel guilty or wrong. For example, if you start a conversation as if you are not feeling valued or paid the right amount, you are putting the person in a defensive mood immediately. They want to feel good about giving. Acknowledge who they are for you and that you appreciate them.
• Higher good: Let them know how what you are asking will benefit them/company. Don't forget it needs to be holistic, benefiting everyone involved.

- Make connection: Keep eye contact, watch their body language, allow time for them to speak.
- Speak into their listening: Everyone is different in how they want to receive information. Some people want a lot of facts and data, some are more interested in a vision for the future, some like more details some less. Be Flexible. Switch course when you see verbal or bodily clues. Make your case in a different way. Relate to people from where they are at.
- Keep it short: Be precise and focused.
- Bring it back: If they divert the subject, tactfully bring it back.
- Speak from the heart: you are not a robot. Be animated and authentic. Let them "see" you.

DON'T:

- Regurgitate to a rehearsed statement. Be in the moment (Breathe)
- Rush: Take your time, slow down. Bringing your attention to your breath will help.
- Waste your words and throw around words to make your point. Speak thoughtfully.
- Get into story. State the facts, not how you felt about them or how others reacted etc. this can take the conversation to a different directions for no reason.
- Blame: them or others. Take responsibility.
- Present your request, as a problem. However, if there is a problem, make sure you have a solution to present as well.

Asking to work from home: Before Covid, for tradition-alists, it was taboo to work from home. The last company I worked for as the head of the creative department, was adamant about hours spent at work and had a swipe in and out system to track employee hours. Therefore, when I asked the president of the company to work from home one day a week, I knew he would have reservations, especially due to the fact that I was in charge of a department. I was prepared to present my case and highlight what was in the interest of the company. I explained to him that on a daily basis I was either pulled into meetings or had people approach me for various questions which took a lot of time and having a day out of the office would help me to focus better for a future vision and do my research. I assured him he wanted me to be in a clear head space and out of the noise of the day to day in the office. And surely, I would come in for import-ant meetings. At first, my boss was reluctant to commit so I suggested we do it on a trial bases to ensure things will go smoothly. I started taking Fridays to work from home during the summer months. It extended naturally into the fall and until the end of my employment there. A bit of give and take helped implement this setup for me. Ultimately it did not take away from my work and helped a great deal with my peace of mind, which in turn helped to boost my attitude and my overall energy as well. A win-win for the company and me.

One of my friends said it wisely; "Do not ask constantly for things. Pick your spots. Don't be a nag. First deliver than ask for things. If you don't get what you asked for, be ready to move on. Don't be attached to an outcome, be flexible and prepared"

If you don't get what you want

"You can't always get what you want, but if you try sometime, you'll find you get what you need"
~ Rolling Stones.

It seems like a harsh statement. But when you don't get what you asked for, it's time to question. Do not get depressed, have low self-esteem, or be angry or sad.

When you question purely, minus all the meanings, emotions and stories you have attached to the situation, you will get the answers you need. **Not getting what you want is an opportunity to re-evaluate your motivations and your desires.

Here is an exercise you can do to practice. It's important to ask in these questions in this specific sequence

1. Why do I think I did not get what I asked for?
2. Are any of these things in my control?
3. What was my motivation in asking for these things?
4. What am I committed to?
5. Can I ask differently?
6. Do I really want something different from what I asked for?
7. What is best for me?

You can always ask again gathering any information from your first meeting and utilizing this to ask differently. It would be beneficial to have a time frame set up with your manager by the end of your meeting. So, ask for example "When can we revisit this? or "What steps do you need to see me take". No is not a no "forever" it is a "not right now" it's an invitation to ask differently, at another time and space.

Throat Chakra (Vishuddi) Meditation for Communication

Lying down on your back in a comfortable posture, relax the whole body. Bring your awareness to your throat. Visualize a black oval, egg shape at the center of the throat. As you breath in and out the black oval gets bigger and bigger eventually surrounding your whole body. Shining black light everywhere. Imagine you are in your mother's womb. As ears develop, the first sound you hear is your mother's heartbeat. Second sound is your own heartbeat. Realization sets in that heartbeat gives support to go manifest your intentions. Allow the oval to become smaller returning back to your throat.

Throat Chakra governs space element. Through space sound vibration travels. Now go deep into your memory and remember the earliest thing you heard as a child that allowed you to evolve your consciousness. Remember within the past 24 hours words you have heard which elevated your consciousness. Remember within the past 24 hours words you have spoken helped evolve someone else's mind space. Notice when you speak words that come from the heart space, they are more powerful, aligning with your purpose.

CHAPTER 6

INFLUENTIAL LEADERSHIP

"You were born with potential.
You were born with goodness & trust.
You were born with ideal & dreams.
You were born with greatness.
You were born with wings.
You are not meant for crawling. So, don't.
You have wings.
Learn to use them and fly"
~ Rumi

Just like the animals, human beings are conditioned to model behavior from our parents. As we grow and take our place in society, parents are replaced by, political figures, heads of states, presidents of the companies, managers, etc...

Not everyone is a natural leader. But everyone has an aspect of their lives in which they assume responsibility to lead others. If you are a parent, you lead by example to your children. If you are taking care of elder parents, you assume a leadership role in making certain decisions with or for them. If you organize an event a social event or gathering, there you would lead too.

An effective leader needs to have a broad vision, the ability to see what is not seen plus willingness to learn and teach others. Regardless of the level of leadership we assume, the success of any department or organization depends on good leadership...

However, in the work environment, some of us have so much talent to put a vision into reality, and are great at working solo, we don't have to deal with the politics of a work environment. Being a leader requires taking responsibility for others, having a commitment to show up authentically and lead by example. Whatever level we are in there is an opportunity to assume leadership and lead with that attitude.

There are many who want to be in the spotlight and maintain sole control. These people think they are leaders; however, the best leaders serve others. Service unlocks purpose, performance and shared responsibility. Many leaders set a great example in terms of their work ethic and discipline, in *how to do*, but fewer, are an example in *how to be*. Leadership is not just about project management. Good leaders need to be excellent at building relationships and trust. Let's break this down.

Qualities of a Great leader are:

1. Self:
    *   Have integrity
    *   Takes responsibility
    *   Knows their strengths and weaknesses
    *   Surrounds themselves with those who support and enhance their qualities
    *   Firm, stable and steady in decision making/ consistency
    *   Have patience
    *   Do not take things personally
    *   Finds Joy in their work
    *   Honest.
    *   Humble. One of my bosses says "Don't be right, be smart"
    *   Does what is necessary.
2. Others:
    *   Sees everyone equally
    *   Knows each individual's talents and gifts
    *   Listens
    *   Not easily mislead from their truth
    *   Caring and supportive in their journey to success.
    *   Fair
    *   Consistent in messaging
    *   Does not expect others to work and feel the same as himself/herself. Finds out about their motivations
    *   Knows how to manage up and down by filtering information and communicating effectively

3. Systems/organization
    *   Inspirational
    *   Sees the big picture
    *   Knows how to navigate in the corporate environment
    *   Has "Time Management" skills,
    *   Knows what is important
    *   Have his/her voice and are not afraid to speak up

A Friend of mine with a very successful career being in the highest positions in multiple investment and wealth management companies told me about two very different bosses he worked under. One, let's call him John, was charismatic, did not spend a lot of time on analysis, but he was decisive, and people got on his bus and went with him. People respected him and liked him. He could be very persuasive. He was a natural born leader. The other one, again, we will call him Jim, was not a natural leader nor charismatic. He even got a lot of criticism for not having confidence and people getting behind him. But he was extremely fair. He was more analytical and detailed as well as focused. He was loyal to a fault. Sometimes loyalty got the best of him. My friend said he became the combination of the two.

At the age of 34 he had 700 people working for him, with most being older and more experienced than him. Being in that situation, he had to develop confidence in people opposed to shoving his authority down their throat. He said in the earlier years he was motivated by being acknowledged and respected but in his later years gaining more confidence in his knowledge and experience, he focused on the job at hand and doing it in the best way possible.

What if you are joining an established organization in a leadership role and are asked to implement change in systems/processes/organizational structure/etc. How do you navigate that?

Change Maker

It's not an easy task to bring change especially to an established organization. But change is possible at every level of an organization. In fact, adaptability to change is vital for the growth of a company! Here are some steps to follow to succeed:

- Identify the problem and the solution: It's easy to point out the problems but having an idea, a solution is what separates you as a leader.
- Package it holistically: Your solution should benefit everyone.
- Engage the most senior person in your idea. You need the support of the top management to implement change.
- Work with others; Be it other directors or departments, to understand the impact and engage them in solutions.
- Know the risk and prepare: Nothing goes smoothly when implementing change. If you understand that

when unexpected problems occur, you can keep calm and deal with the situation.

- Own it: Don't run away from the responsibility.
- Keep your energy and focus.
- Keep the vision alive: Don't forget; we are forgetful!
- Encourage others to share their vision: You don't know what you don't know! Be open to learn so you can improve the solution.
- Be flexible, know when to let go and allow compromise when your idea has run its course.

I walked into a work environment without organization and separateness. Meetings I attended first were the war of the titans everyone staying in their corner and in a defensive mode. Although everyone seemed to work hard to get their job done, there was an underline hostility in dynamics and general disconnect.

After meeting with all individuals which took my first week in the office and attending their seldom meetings, for another few weeks, I quickly realized trying to repair "what is" would be like putting a bandage, I had to wipe a clean slate, make a plan and org chart to start all over again utilizing the talent and creating the clear communication channels. I got support and green light from my superiors to do that. But this had to be done delicately and with partnership of the Managers within the department. So, they can champion the idea within their channels. The first action to take was to engage them into this new idea. This was the real work. To engage, get to know them, to let them know they are seen and valued so they will start to listen.

Also, to admit that we follow the plan, but plan is not always the perfect plan, we allow the input of everyone as we implement and adopt to the circumstances and stay flexible. So, plan can be ever evolving as it is necessary. This approach has proven to be the right one as department got streamlined, people become less stressed, and company grew exponentially within the next years.

Pranayama for Leadership

Prana refers to movement or breath with direction. ("pra" = forth, "an" = movement, breath) It's the life energy. Pranayama refers to mastery of this energy. There are several techniques presented in yoga some to extend the exhale and some as inhale hold "kumbhaka" which helps with balancing the two hemispheres of the brain which aids in harmony of all organs and systems of the body as well as releasing tension due to false perception of who we are.

A lot of people breathe using the intercoastal and scalene muscles rather than the diaphragm. This has terrible consequences; lack of oxygen, too much CO_2 tilts our physiology in the favor or sympathetic nervous system drive. In other words, this means we are either fight, flight or freeze mode never rest, digest, and recover state. This increases anxiety and becomes a vicious cycle.

Ujjayi breathing is a great practice to combat this habitual breathing pattern. Ujjayi means "victorious breath" "u" refers to the upward direction. It suggests an upward moving force of prana. In this way we centralize the breath which creates a steadiness in the mind.

To practice, with mouth close, constrict your throat (epiglottis or soft palate) to a point that the sound of the breath becomes like an ocean wave or the sound of Darth Vader from Star Wars. Once you get comfortable apply this to both inhale and exhale and breath this way only through the nose. Keep your breathing long and engage mind in the sound of the breath.

CHAPTER 7

WHAT IS SUCCESS

You were born from a ray of God's majesty
and have the blessings of a good star.
Why suffer at the hands of things that don't exist?
Come, return to the root of the root of your Self.
~ Rumi

Most of us are taught that being successful will make us happy and that success is defined as having things! Monetary gains: a house, car, etc. and advancement at the workplace: an important title, people reporting to you, getting recognition. Therefore, everyone who achieves these things should be happy! Is that really the case, though?

The feeling we get from "having" things maybe "pride", "admiration or envy of others" "being better than" etc. You can see these are me-centered emotional experiences, only inviting more egoistic activities, therefore creating a world around "I and what is mine" However, "ownership" does not necessarily equate happiness. Living with this perspective, makes one bounded by likes and dislikes. This duality is the cause of dissatisfaction and unhappiness, in an unending race running after what is wanted and avoiding at all costs what is not wanted. This is maybe why we hear about so many brilliant and rich people having depression, anxiety, sadness and relying on drugs to "take the edge off".

If the measurement of success is happiness, and if happiness does not come from the material world, then how do we find it? There's a story of a deer told in Yoga; The musk deer in India has a very enchanting smell, it is used to make perfumes. The deer smells this enticing aroma and does not know where its coming from. He searches for his entire life to find the source of this beautiful smell. He runs through forest after forest searching for the source of the smell, eventually dyeing of exhaustion. Are we also perhaps mistakenly looking for satisfaction outside of us?

All Pleasures have a beginning and an end.-. Marketing people tell us constantly, that we are missing something. If we have this or that, then we will be happy. But when we get whatever "that" is, we realize the euphoric feeling is short lived. So, we chase after the next thing to find ourselves once again in the same situation with dissatisfaction. External things through contact with senses do not give us happiness. They ultimately give birth to misery

These are the three scenarios in which desires lead to suffering:

1. You want something, you don't know how to get it, and you never get it.
2. You want something, you get it, but then you lose it.
3. You want something, you get it, but then it does not live up to your expectations.

You may have experienced a feeling of success as being perhaps the youngest manager, only female in the boardroom, with a new title, or more money. but these scenarios also come with their own set of challenges and frustrations. How, then do we pull ourselves out of the conditioned way of being; this chasing for happiness outside of ourselves? How do we succeed in such a way that gives us true satisfaction and happiness?

Here are 10 principles to live by at work (and in life in general) that will lead you to true satisfaction and contentment:

- *Higher Vision*: Having an overarching intention at any given moment will allow you to stop focusing on small inconveniences and see a larger picture.
- *Know yourself:* Notice societal and familial conditioning and see underneath it all, who you really are and what makes you truly happy and satisfied. Then move in that direction. When you do things from the heart, there's no way not to succeed.
- *Be who you are*: Don't try to be like anyone else. You are unique and special. Do not try to conform,

duplicate, or measure against anyone. When you stop comparing yourself with another, or let others, such as marketing people, your family, or societal norms to decide who you should be, in order to be successful, then you can truly explore who you are. In this way, you will avoid the pitfalls of giving up, opting out via self-indulgence and addiction.

- *Celebrate small victories:* What you accomplish each day, an accumulation of consecutive small victories will bring you to a future moment of success

- *Be patient:* Wait and observe. Allow time for things to come to fruition.

- *Perseverance:* Cultivate a drive that you will not give up easy. Keep trying in a different way. My husband always says he does not hear a "no" when people say so. He only hears "please ask me in a different way". (Yes, he gets his way most of the time ☺)

- *No attachments:* Attachments almost always cloud our vision and ability to see what is beyond what seems possible. When we go after victories and try to avoid failures, we soon realize that the very thing we try to avoid is what is needed for our growth. When we stop worrying about the outcome, we free ourselves to embrace and learn from our experiences.

- *Be of service*: Do your work for the benefit of others or a greater cause, not just to build your ego. My old boss was an example of this when he said the community services he is doing through his organizations and others was what gave him satisfaction and more energy to do his work in the corporate space.

- ***Build a community:*** When you have an intention for building a community through your work, you get out of the world of "me, myself and I" and start caring for others. In this way you will create a support system for yourself as well.

- ***Single focus:*** Stephen Covey wrote in his book "7 Habits of Highly Effective People"; "Main thing is to keep the main thing the main thing" Keep a singular focus and don't let yourself be distracted by the noise. Remember your purpose in every step.

STORY OF ARJUNA & EYE OF THE BIRD*
(From Mahabharata)

When Dronacarya was teaching archery to his students, he once asked them to shoot a bird in the tree by aiming at its eye. He called them one by one and showing the bird, he asked them what they saw. Everyone except Arjuna, said that they saw the tree, the branches, the bird etc. and so everyone missed the target.

Arjuna had been practicing archery day and night and was the best archer among the students of Dronacarya. So, when Arjuna's turn came Drona inquired him as follows.

Drona: "What do you see?"
Arjuna: "I see the eye of the bird"
Drona: "Do you see the tree?"
Arjuna: "No"
Drona: "Do you see the branch?"
Arjuna: "No"
Drona: "Do you see the bird?"
Arjuna: "No"
Drona: "Then what else do you see, Arjuna?"
Arjuna: "Nothing.

Saying so Arjuna released the arrow and it hit the target straight.

Lord Krishna Himself declares in Bhagavad Gita verse 2.41:

vyavasaayaatmikaa buddhir / ekeha kuru-nandana
bahu-shaakhaa hy anantaash ca / buddhayo
'vyavasaayinaam

"Those who are on this path are resolute in purpose, and their aim is one. O beloved child of the Kurus, the intelligence of those who are irresolute is many-branched."

The idea of success is ever fluid. It is not measured by having things but by having experiences, cultivating love and kindness, and sharing a joyful outlook no matter what comes your way. One of my clients described success as "feeling comfortable in your own skin". Another client described being successful as the joyfulness she experiences as she walks into her office every morning.

On the other hand, a mentor of mine in his later years said that he wished he was a better parent, that he could have been closer to his children. But he was always busy at work, traveling, or when he was at home, he was on a "very important call", always making excuses. He said he realized looking back, what made him successful in material sense was not the courage to do things, as he originally thought, it was the fear of failure, being poor, not to be able to provide for his family.

Fear of failure gets in the way of finding success. Nothing is permanent and invariably you are going to fail sometimes and not do things completely right. Even believing you can achieve perfection is an illusion which can be detrimental to your success. Some may argue that perfectionism can be self-motivating, but ultimately, it's harmful for your mental health and well-being.

Perfection in Action

"As you start to walk on the way,
Way appears"

I have worked with many clients who have been held back only because of their own "perfectionism" and sometimes the projection onto others. They justify their non-action with thoughts such as:

"I can't speak out until what I have to say is perfect."
"I can't send in the project on time, it's not yet perfect."
"I will not promote that person yet they are not performing perfectly."

Where does this idea of "being perfect" comes from? In essence, fear of failure, or looking inadequate is simply a cover up to protect the false ego. The unwillingness to try and make mistakes for the sake of "looking good" only puts more limitations on your growth.

The illusion of perfection is so enticing that we are willing to not take a step forward even when it appears right in front of us. The hyper critical lens we constantly subject ourselves and others to does not help our personal and professional growth or the growth of the organization.

Let me present to you an idea of "Perfection in Action," rather than "Perfection as a destination".

Perfection in Action is:

- Being satisfied with the effort put towards the intended goal: This is most difficult for a "perfectionist." It requires one lenses to focus on the present and detach from results. Being result oriented is important but being attached to a certain outcome will hinder the potential of the project or the organization.

- Being Flexible: If the vision is too rigid – the "either my way or no way" philosophy – it will almost always end up in failure as nothing ever goes the way you plan. Every mistake or a wrong turn is a learning opportunity.

- Being focused and not all over the place: Wherever your attention goes, energy flows. When you try to do too many things at the same time, your energy disperses, and your faculties are not fully channeled to doing the task on hand. By giving your attention to the task without having many distractions will have you finish it faster and more accurately.

- Simplify: Not wasting time and energy going down the rabbit holes. Sometimes it is important to consider all avenues and think of all possible scenarios if they are contributing to the solution but not at the expense of people's time and energies or your own.

- Being consistent: Alignment of word and action is very important. "I say what I will do, and I will do what I say"
- Appreciating people's work and efforts: Gratitude is the key to satisfaction. When you operate from gratefulness, you realize the value of what is right and not just focus on what is wrong. In this way you can concentrate on what is working as a step towards finding solutions. Pointing out what is not working is very easy for people. Those who offer solutions have this understanding.
- Criticizing without being judgmental helps create a healthy discussion toward worthy actions.
- Apologizing when necessary.
- Don't burn your bridges with others: You never know when you will meet the person in another setting. Your reputation is how people remember you.

Perfectionism suggests that you are in control and know everything. But in reality, you don't always need to know how and where ideas will take you, but you need to take the step and receive what comes along the way. Strength of character is not staying rigid in your ideas and principles, but on the contrary, being flexible and always able to deal with what life throws your way.

Pranayama for Physical and Mental Balance

Nadi Shodhana: This is a great technique for balancing and harmonizing "vata" (excess of air and space, managing all movements of mind and body) known as "alternate nostril breathing"

It is a rhythmic, soothing, and grounding practice. It is excellent for releasing physical and mental tension and supporting a clear mind, while reducing stress.

Practice is done with the aid of fingers closing right and left nostril alternately. Air is inhaled through the left nostril, pause and exhale through the right nostril. Repeat with inhale through right nostril, pause and exhale through left nostril. This completes one cycle, and you can repeat as many cycles as you can.

CHAPTER 8

SELF-CARE NOT
SELF INDULGENCE

"When I run after what I think I want, my days are a
furnace of stress and anxiety; if I sit in my own place of
patience, what I need flows to me, and without pain.
From this I understand that what I want also wants me,
is looking for me and attracting me."
~ Rumi

As we connected more with the invention of smart phones, it blurred the lines between work and personal lives. Once the idea of separating work and personal life became a negotiating balance, the idea of work-life balance started to become more fluid as we collectively started working from home during Covid. Companies started investing more on wellness for their employees, some following the trend for appearance's sake, some more heartedly. The organizations who embraced the idea of wellness in the workplace understood that in fact potential of a company lies in the potential of each individual.

It's not easy or ideal to make important decisions or think creatively, while under stress and anxiety. Stress and anxiety are signs that your energy is depleted. Self-care means attending to one's physical and mental health (without medical or professional consultation). It means recharging your inner batteries to give you greater endurance and more energy. It's self regulation, or as we call it in yoga therapy, "having resilience". Self-care is mistakenly portrayed at times, as "having drinks with friends", "taking a bubble bath", "shopping" or "eating sweets" etc. What is wrong with a bubble bath? Absolutely nothing, but if you are unable to subdue the mind chatter will a bubble bath suffice? If you wake up with a hang-over, does a drink suffice? If you go shopping, will the joy of having something new last? The answer to all these questions is no.

What we think is self-care may not be…

Self-care is not self-indulgence or escapism. If you are checking out and not participating in your life, *you have not been taking care of yourself;* if you are unable to control your emotions and your reactions, *you have not been taking care of yourself.* If you are triggered easily, feel anxiety and fear constantly, this is a telling sign that y*ou have not been taking care of yourself.*

Self-care is not a fad or fashion, another thing to check on your to-do list. Self-care requires a pause to allow the mind to slow down, and not constantly react to the outer stimuli it receives. This allows your true intelligence to emerge.

Self-care is the act of caring for your Self and being your best advocate ALL THE TIME.

How to Care for Your Self:

1. *Sleep well:*

   • Leave your phone, turned off, outside the bedroom
   • Stop eating/drinking water at least 3 hours before going to sleep
   • Go to sleep before midnight
   • Don't jump out of bed with the alarm or as soon as you open your eyes. Allow yourself to rise slowly and notice your breath

2. *Establish a Morning routine*: Your mind needs to be cared for just the way you take care of your physical body, routinely, by brushing your teeth, taking a shower etc. It's important to mentally release the previous day and night, when energy separates from the body and has experiences, moving through space and time, which we call dreaming.

3. *Take time off:* Make sure you allow yourself to take a day of during your week from work and daily responsibilities to be outdoors, in nature, to take a walk, hike, watch an uplifting movie, or read a good book. Do an activity that makes you happy. Empty the mind, spend time alone and direct the mind toward things that uplift your spirit.

> *I asked one of my mentors where he gets his energy, he said he never is very needy for outside or for too much input. He quoted this from a book; "Wisdom of Life" of Schopenhauer: "The more one has within themselves the less they require from outside"*

4. *Stay away from negative people*: Being around negative dialog will either exhaust you or create more fire (anger, frustration, worry etc.) in the mind, which ends up burning your energies and exhausting you. Choose who you want to be with, carefully.

5. *Eat well:* "You are what you eat!" In Ayurveda*, Science of Holistic medicine, it is explained, how to balance food according to one's dosha * and physical needs.

6. Pay attention to what you put in your mouth. Your body is your temple. You want your temple to be clean and spotless. Eat clean, healthy food. This does not mean to avoid all the things that you love but do it in moderation. Self-care means balance!

7. *Focus:* A focused mind is a happy mind. Stop trying to do too many things at once. Do one thing at a time and do it well.

It's hard to do this sometimes at work. Multi-tasking is expected and rewarded but try not to take a call when you are meeting with someone (it's more respectful to the person you are with, after all). Schedule your meetings to have breathing time in between to get up, walk, stretch your legs, drink water, go to the bathroom. I can't count how many times people, including myself, forget to go to the bathroom or eat during the workday which is very unhealthy and exhausting. I will repeat it: Do one thing at a time and do it well.

Most people don't understand their true power lies in releasing resistance. We are taught struggle, sacrifice and hardship is necessary for a reward of great abundance. But that very struggle we involve ourselves in, for success and abundance, works against us. This is why yogis present a path of much less resistance

We need to learn to breathe, rather than resist; relax, rather than try hard, release, rather than be attached. Emotions and judgements we attach to experiences are the production of the mind, but your true power is experienced only from inside.

Let go of what is not necessary or helpful,
Let go of old habits and stories,
Let go of negativity and envy,
Let go of the worry,
Relax...relax...relax...

Some ideas for a morning self-care routine are:

- Stretch and Strengthen: Take 5-10 min to stretch and if you regularly go to the gym in the morning, you are on to something. Between 6 am-10 am is the Kapha* time, giving us great strength and endurance of the day. It's nature's way of calling us to get up and get moving. If you don't, try some strengthening practices.

  Example of a morning yoga practice:

  Sun-Salutations:
  Start standing then forward fold,
  Plank – with optional push ups
  Cobra
  Downward dog
  Lunges on both legs
  Chair pose or wall/sits
  Headstand – if it's in your practice
  Childs pose

- Breathe: Take a few minutes to bring your awareness to your breath. When we connect to our breath, it calms down the sympathetic nervous system almost immediately, staying in that space for an extended time will calm the mind.

> • Create an intention for your day. When mind is calm, we can connect to our deeper intellect and wisdom to get more creative and clearer on our choices and responses to whatever life brings on.

Burn out

Having personally been through and seen the many examples of burn out all around me, it is an undeniable <u>fact</u> of corporate life. Burn out is like taking a hot power vinyasa or a spin class and holding your breath while pushing through. You cannot sustain that type of practice or a work style in the long run. When you are non-stop pushing through your day from project to project, meeting to meeting, one spread sheet to another, without proper breaks and regulated time for sleep, nutrition, and relaxation, you are in constant fight or flight modes. In other words, you are operating within the automatic sympathetic nervous system, which is responsible for the body's unconscious actions, operating from the lower mind, stimulating the body's fight and flight responses.

During most of my career I would run out of my house to work without having any breakfast and meet first thing in the morning, some adversity; an employee in distress, a meeting with intensity.

Then I would go from one meeting to another making decisions along the way. Lunch was a quick soup/salad at my desk while someone in my office was pouring their frustrations or asking for feedback on their proposal. The consistent stomach pain which took me to the ER one morning was the warning sign my body tried to communicate to me. For a long time, I did not listen. One day through self-study, I realized how much stress I was putting on my body and mind without sufficient fuel and energy, for the sake of "not wasting time" and "getting things done". I learned to say no to lunch meetings so I could go outside and take a walk and eat in peace. This was a step in the right direction to clearing my mind and supporting my body. I also realized the key for me was to get to the office a little earlier to have some breakfast and quiet time (admittedly while checking emails to prepare for the day ahead, but still a victory over the past) My stomach pains slowly disappeared.

When you stop caring:

I hear when people complain about having stopped caring about their job, they are either;

a. Burned out – if that is the case, then you can re-read the self-care chapter to see where you have not been taking care of yourself and how to adopt some healthier choices into your daily routine.

b. Stop growing – When you do things repetitively, you stop seeing the possibility. Thus, you miss the opportunity to go deeper, understand better, to grow. Solution to this is not necessarily to have a new job, but to have new lenses in which you see through your work. In this way you may see something you have not seen before.

c. Need to let go – There's an upside to stop caring if you are an HSP* "a highly sensitive person "or a "perfectionist". Sometimes in relaxing and releasing attachments to how you need things to be, you can free yourself and do better at work

---

EXERCISE

Let's try this: Sit comfortably and close your eyes (to gather the attention from outside and to direct to yourself, often eyes are the most pulling of our senses, closing them helps this process to be faster) Notice 4 parts of your breath. There is an inhalation with a split second of retention at the top of the inhale, followed by an exhalation with a split second of retention at the bottom of the exhale. Notice as you pause at the top of the inhale there's a certain amount of tension and exertion builds in the whole body, heart muscles get slightly constrained, diaphragm contracts and creates a dome like shape, till you exhale when at the bottom of the exhale the whole body relaxes, tensions get released in the muscles of the heart, and the diaphragm flattens. As you continue to watch your breath, include a mantra (*) such as "I choose to relax now", "I give myself permission to surrender, now", "I am resilient" or "even though I am under stress and anxiety, I know it's temporary"

CHAPTER 9

SPIRITUALIZING YOUR WORK / RAISE YOUR VIBRATION

"You were born with potential. You were born with goodness & trust. You were born with ideals & dreams. You were born with greatness. You were born with wings. You are not meant for crawling. So, don't. You have wings. Learn to use them and fly."
~ Rumi

In essence, we are spiritual beings. Because of that we are not satisfied by material objects. When we have a greater purpose, a "why" to our work, we are motivated and more connected to the work we are doing and to one another. In this way we can spiritualize our work. This requires spiritualizing our mind and intelligence in other words raising our vibration.

HOW TO RAISE YOUR VIBRATION:

Socially:

1. Do not harm: This is an easy one! Not only on a physical level but also emotional and mental levels. Don't intentionally go after another and try to hurt them, don't shut down people's ideas without giving some consideration. Non harming does not only apply to others but yourself. Negative self-talk, neglecting your health and well-being are all part of this principle.

2. Tell the truth: Even when it's uncomfortable, telling what is true to you without judgement, blame or criticizing, is the most powerful way of living. This practice eliminates the need to conform or defend, rather, it supports your individuality.

3. Do not steal: People's space, time, energy, ideas...

4. Use your energy wisely: Choose moderation in work, entertainment, rest, eating and drinking. Regulating your activities will create abundant energy.

5. Do not hoard: Choose to free yourself from attachment and greed.

"Let your concern be with the action alone and never the fruits of action. Do not let the results of your action be your motive and do not be attached to inaction"
~ Krishna in BG

Personally:

1. Keep it clean: Yes, I went there. I have had body odor issues that became such an issue it led me to have a conversation about it with the respected party. Not just your personal hygiene but your workplace has to be clean and without clutter. This gives you breathing room to get creative and get to work, it also makes an impression as someone who respects his/her body and space. Also watch your bad habits, you can always refine your lifestyle from what you eat to how you talk to yourself.

2. Practice Contentment: It is not "when" you will be happy (when I have the position, the job, the relationship, the house etc.) it's finding the feeling in every moment by accepting and appreciating what you have, now.

3. Nothing is permanent. We experience many emotions from joy to disappointment, but all of these are passing emotions. No one is only happy or only miserable, all the time! Searching for external conditions to be ideal will only lead us to more desires, which than becomes attachments and eventually anger, sadness, frustration when they are not met. Whatever situation you find yourself in now was something you chose at some point. You have the power to change it, maintain it or leave it.

4. Find Discipline: Self-discipline is the way to freedom. It requires control of the mind. Mind is

easily distracted and constantly seeks to attach itself to objects and events which are "preferred" which then creates duality in the mind. This is the cause of suffering. To bring the mind to a place where there's peace regardless of the circumstances and events can be achieved only trough self-discipline.

5. Learn, about the subject matter and about yourself: Illusion of knowing, is a big obstacle to learning. It's like trying to see the world through a dark veil. Limited and mostly unclear. Benjamin Franklin said "We are all born ignorant, but one must work hard to remain stupid" attitude of humbleness is a key to lifting the veil.

6. Surrender: Do what you must and then leave the rest to the universe. It's not easy for most of us control freaks to "let go" and "surrender". It sounds like "losing control" but on the contrary, surrendering requires self-discipline and humility. Knowing what must be done and when to release control and allow others to contribute is opposite of living in a "I and mine" world. Nothing is yours. You are not the doer. You are not the controller, but you must do what you committed to the best of your ability with the right intention. Trust that whatever happens has a reason and that is the jewel, not to dwell on things not going your way or the way you have planned. But to inquire about how to work with the end result to find a new opportunity, a new way. Things will get tough and at times out of your control. These are opportune

moments to shake you out of the comfort zone you have created, to put you into action, to excite you. Overall, the most important thing is to find humility and kindness. And keep your relationships healthy.

On December 11, 1995, a dust explosion in one of the hoppers used to produce Polartec destroyed three of the Malden factory's buildings and causing 40% damage to the whole plant. The fire happened during the companies off season leading to minimized losses, though at the time it was the largest property damage fire loss in the history of Massachusetts affecting workers. Lawrence MA was already experiencing a downward economy due to many other companies leaving to find cheaper labor elsewhere and many residents were worried about the loss of another factory. The fire injured 36 people and placed 2700 jobs at risk. The fire was later ruled an "industrial accident."

CEO Aaron Feuerstein made the decision overnight to quickly rebuild. He extended the pay and benefits of his employees while the factory was being rebuilt. Rebuilding was completed on September 14, 1997, leaving 70 employees still displaced.

Though ultimately Feuerstein's choices may have led to the insolvency of the company and the loss of nearly all the jobs that Feuerstein was trying to preserve, he received praise for his choice to de-prioritize the profitability of his company. * He was one of the inspirational leaders for my old boss who told me the story.

**Bhagavat Gita says "There are 2 types of intelligent men. the one in material activities for sense gratification, for gain (wealth, power, recognition, so on) and the other who is introspective and awake to the cultivation of self-realization. The thoughtful man finds transcendental pleasure in gradual advancement of spiritual practice, whereas materialistic man, being asleep to self-realization, dreams of varieties of sense pleasure, feeling sometimes happy, sometimes distressed in his sleeping condition. The introspective man is always indifferent to materialistic happiness and distress he goes on with his activities, undisturbed by material reaction"

There is no happiness without peace. Peaceful mind is fixed in worthy causes and understanding their conditioning, not focused on altering outward circumstances.

Most of us started our careers for the right reasons and attitude. But sometimes we get addicted to the lifestyle, to money, to a title and lose what is really important, along the way. Start questioning now: "what are my motivations?" "What legacy I would like to have?" "What makes me happy?" and "what is in the way of having a happy, fulfilled, joyful life?"

When we pause and start asking these questions, the answers will become apparent.

Sankalpa

Sankalpa refers to heartfelt desire. This term comes from the Sanskrit root "san" meaning "a connection with the highest truth" It is a short phrase or sentence, clear, sharp, and positive to bring a positive change in an aspect of your life.

Unlike a goal, which implies achieving something in a temporary way, creating a daily, monthly, yearly or life sankalpa focuses the mind towards the heart's higher intention. Before starting your day, first thing in the morning have a pause and repeat a Sankalpa mentally. This will help align the energies of the day to your benefit.

Basak Gunaydin

* Wikipedia

**Srila Prabhupada's Commentary on BG Verse 2.69

BONUS MATERIAL

This section offers more detail explanations, as well as the sources, for the various philosophical and practical ideas established by Yoga. I hope this is helpful for those who might like to delve deeper into yoga philosophy.

Sources and Material inspires this book

My yoga teacher Yogi Charu introduced me to some of the most revered texts of yoga, including Yoga Sutras of Patanjali, Bhagavat Gita and Srimad Bhagavatam. Specifically, "Bhagavat Gita," which is one of the 18 chapters of epic "Mahabharata," believed to be written about 5,000 years ago, informs us how to be great leaders and engage in life embodying yogic principles and lifestyle.

Yoga sutras of Patanjali, written about 2,000 years ago, is a road map to enlightenment. It is presented in an intellectual and profound way that the average seeker can follow.

Srimad Bhagavatam (or Bhagavata Purana), written around the 8th and 10th century CE, introduces a wide range of topics including cosmology, astronomy, genealogy, geography, yoga, culture.

These ancient books show the meaning of life, purpose and why we want to live our lives in a certain manner, to experience freedom from material conditioning.

Chapter 1

Yoga: Sanskrit word for "union" originates from the root "Yuj" yoke or "yuktena" to be joined. Implying the union, connectedness of the mind, body, spirit. Yoga philosophy is a principle in which supporting spirituality and a way of life, regardless of a religious affiliation.

Yamas & Niyamas: Moral conducts or right living.

Yamas: Translated as "moral discipline" or "restraint". Yamas are the principles to help guide our interactions with our environment. These principles are:

1. Ahimsa (non-harming in thought, word, and action)
2. Satya (truthfulness, honesty towards yourself and others)
3. Asteya (non-stealing of time, energy, material objects)
4. Brahmacharya (right usage of energy)

Niyamas: Personal conducts, habits for good living

1. Aparigraha (non-greed or non-hoarding)
2. Saucha (cleanliness)
3. Santosha (contentment)
4. Tapas (Discipline)
5. Svadhyaya (self study)
6. Isvara Pranidhana (surrender to a higher being or contemplating of the higher source)

Chapter 2

This is Introduction of Light on Yoga:

"Along with ahimsa(non-violence) go abhaya (freedom from fear) and akroda (freedom from anger). Freedom from fear comes only to those who lead a pure life. The yogi fears none and none need fear him because he is purified by the study of the Self. Fear grips a man and paralyses him. He is afraid of the future, the unknown and the unseen. He is afraid that he might lose his means of livelihood, wealth, or reputation. But the greatest fear is that of death. The yogi knows that he is different from his body, which is a temporary house for his spirit...."

Chapter 3

Bhagavat Gita: ("Song of God" or "Song of the Lord") is among the most important religious texts of Hinduism and easily the best known. Describing a conversation between two friends, Krishna & Arjuna, on the meaning of life and how to live a life powerfully.

Sangha: Association, community, assemble of like-minded individuals, practicing, sharing, evolving together

Chapter 4

4 types of people Bhagavat Gita Chapter 7. Verse 14

Karma: The sum of a person's actions in this and previous states of existence, viewed as deciding their fate in future existences. Every action causes a reaction.

Gunas: Modes of nature. Bhagavat Gita Chapter 14 Verses 1-27

1. Sattva (goodness)
2. Rajas (passion)
3. Tamas (dullness)

Sat cit Ananda: Satcitananda (सच्चिदानन्द) is a compounded Sanskrit word consisting of "*sat*", "*chit*", and "*ananda*", Condition of the soul: Eternal (truth), full of knowledge and bliss.

Chapter 5

Koshas: In Eastern philosophy, the *koshas* are considered the energetic layers of your body. Each layer is made of increasingly finer grades of energy. The five progressively subtler bodies that compose our personality are described in a yoga classic called the *Taittiriya Upanishad*
These 5 layers are:

1. Anamaya Kosha (Physical layer)
2. Pranayama Kosha (Energetic layer)

3. Manomaya Kosha (Mind)
4. Vgyanamaya Kosha (Intellect)
5. Anandamaya Kosha (soul)

Chapter 8

Ayurveda: Ayurveda, **a natural system of medicine**, originated in India more than 3,000 years ago. The term Ayurveda is derived from the Sanskrit words ayur (life) and veda (science or knowledge). Thus, Ayurveda translates to knowledge of life. (www.hopkinsmedicine.org)

Dosha: Unique combination of five elements (earth, water, fire, air, ether) in the universe and in our being, which is responsible for a person's physiological, mental, and emotional well-being.

- Kapha dosha is the combination of earth and water elements. Its qualities are heavy, dense, and steady.
- Pita Dosha is the combination of the fire and water elements. Its qualities are quick, sharp, warm
- Vata dosha is the combination of air and either element. Its qualities are dry, cool, light

Mantra: (Sanskrit) an incantation with words of power, a sacred message. Comprised of word "Man = to think, manas = mind" and "tra = protector"

INDEX

5. Communication is Everything
- Challenging People and How to Deal with Them
- The Art of Arguing
- Asking for What You Want

6. Influential Leadership
- Change maker

7. What is Success?
"Meaning of success and 10 principles to live by that will lead you to satisfaction and happiness at the workplace"
- Perfection in Action

8. Self-care not self-indulgence
"What is self-care and how to care for one's self in the workplace?"
- Burn out
- When you stop caring

9. Art of Spiritualizing your work
"How to stay inspired by your work"

TOPICAL INDEX

❦

ABOUT THE AUTHOR

Basak **Gunaydin,** Turkish-American, C-IAYT (Internationally licensed Yoga Therapist), 500 E-RYT (Experienced Registered Yoga Teacher), YACEP (Yoga Alliance Continuing Education Provider), Textile Engineer.

After 30 years of a Corporate Career and 10 years of teaching yoga, meditation and breathwork simultaneously, Basak moved from her position as a Vice President of Design of a Sports Apparel Company to a full time Yoga Therapist and a teacher role Since 2020 right before Covid, after a pilgrimage to India. She organizes and leads international retreats, teaches yoga meditation and breath classes and wellness workshops in the corporate space with companies such as IBM, Wework, several Law and Investment firms, both online and in person. She works with private clients in a therapeutic and coaching capacity.

Basak lives in New York City with her husband, Jonathan and her beloved Pamuk.

www.ingramcontent.com/pod-product-compliance
Lightning Source LLC
Chambersburg PA
CBHW051545170526
45165CB00002B/888